Con

C000138563

Showing and Telling in Fiction

A BUSY WRITER'S GUIDE

Marcy Kennedy

Tongue Untied Communications
ONTARIO, CANADA

Marcy Kennedy
marcykennedy@gmail.com
www.marcykennedy.com

Book Layout ©2013 BookDesignTemplates.com
Edited by Christopher Saylor

Showing and Telling in Fiction/ Marcy Kennedy. —1st ed.
ISBN 978-0-9920371-6-1

Why a Busy Writer's Guide?

Every how-to-become-a-better-writer list includes studying craft. Years ago, as a new writer, I took that advice to heart but found that many craft books didn't give me the detailed, in-the-trenches coverage of a topic I needed. They included a lot of beautifully written prose and theory without explaining how to practically apply the principles, or they gave numerous examples but didn't explain how to replicate those concepts in my own work.

I ended up buying three or four books on the same topic to understand it fully and get the balance of theory and practice I was looking for. I spent more time studying craft than writing, and all the exercises in the books seemed to take me away from my story rather than helping me work directly on it. For the modern writer who also needs to blog and be on social media, who might be juggling a day job, and who still wants time to see their family or friends, that's a problem. Do you know anyone who doesn't have more commitments then they're able to handle already without adding "study the writing craft" on top of it?

We're busy. We're tired. We're overworked. We love writing, but often wonder if it's worth the sacrifices we're making for it. We know we're headed down the fast track to burning out, but don't know what we can do differently.

I wrote the *Busy Writer's Guide* series to help you fast-track the learning process. I felt that writers needed a fluff-free guide that would give them the detailed coverage of a topic they required while also respecting their time. I want you to be able to spend the majority of your writing time actually writing, so that you can set aside your computer and enjoy the people and experiences that make life worth living.

Each *Busy Writer's Guide* is intended to serve as an accelerated master's class in a topic. I'll give you enough theory so that you can understand why things work and why they don't, and enough examples to see how that theory looks in practice. I'll also provide tips and exercises to help you take it to the pages of your own story with an editor's-eye view.

This *Busy Writer's Guide* also includes special appendices. If you understand the concepts in the rest of the book, you can skip the appendices without feeling like you're missing something essential. I've included them because I felt they'd be helpful for people who wanted a little extra help with a very tricky element of the writing craft.

My goal, as always, is for you to come away a stronger writer, with a stronger piece of work, than when you came in.

CHAPTER ONE

Defining Showing and Telling

You've heard the advice *show, don't tell* until you can't stand to hear it anymore. Yet all writers still seem to struggle with it.

I think there are three reasons for this.

The first is that this isn't an absolute rule. Telling isn't always wrong. It doesn't always lead to weak, flat writing. Showing vs. telling is all about balance.

The second is that we lack a clear way of understanding the difference between showing and telling.

The third is that we're told *show, don't tell*, but we're often left without practical ways to know how and when to do that, and how and when not to.

So that's what this book is about. I'm going to give you ways to understand showing and telling, and I'll identify some practical ways to figure out when to change telling to showing and when to leave it as is.

WHAT DO WE MEAN BY SHOWING?

Showing happens when we let the reader experience things for themselves, through the perspective of the characters. Jeff Gerke, former owner of Marcher Lord Press, explains showing in one simple question: Can the camera see it?[1]

While I love that way of looking at it, we'd really have to ask can the camera see it, hear it, smell it, touch it, taste it, or think it? (And that would be a strange camera.) Because of that, I prefer to think about showing as being in a *Star Trek* holodeck.

For those of you who aren't as nerdy as I am, a holodeck is a virtual reality room where users can act as a character in a story, which is fully projected using photons and force fields. You can play Jane Eyre or *Twilight*'s Bella or Lee Child's Jack Reacher.

What the user experiences is what they can see, hear, touch, taste, or smell. In holodecks, you can smell things and you can eat or drink "replicated" food. It's a completely immersive experience. To the holodeck user, the experience seems real in all respects. And if you turn the holodeck safety systems off, you can be injured or even die.

When you're faced with deciding whether something is showing or telling, ask yourself this question: If this were a holodeck program, would I be able to experience this?

Let's take a couple examples and test them out. A straightforward one first.

Kate realized she'd locked her keys in the car.

---

[1] Jeff Gerke, *The First 50 Pages* (Cincinnati: Writer's Digest Books, 2011), 40.

Now, you're standing in the holodeck. What do you experience?

...Nothing. We can't see "realized." We don't know how she knows her keys are locked in the car. Anything we might visualize is something we've had to add because the author didn't. There's no picture here.

Here's one possible showing version...

> Kate yanked on the car door handle. The door didn't budge, and her keys dangled from the ignition. "Dang it!"

You don't have to tell us Kate realized her keys were locked inside her car because we're right there with her. We see her figure it out.

Let's take a more challenging example. This time you're in the holodeck, playing the character of Linda. (Remember that, since you're Linda, you can hear her thoughts, as well as see, smell, hear, taste, and feel what she does.)

First the "telling" version.

> Linda stood at the edge of the Grand Canyon. Though her head spun from the height, she was amazed by the grandeur of it and felt a sense of excitement. Finally she'd taken a big step toward overcoming her fear of heights.

What do you physically experience in the holodeck? Only the Grand Canyon. If you don't know what the Grand Canyon looks like, you can't see even that. None of the rest can appear around you. None of it is her thoughts. They're all abstractions. What does being amazed by the grandeur look like? What does excitement feel like? What does her fear of heights feel like?

If we're in the holodeck, it's going to play out something more like this...

> Linda gripped the damp metal railing that ringed the horseshoe-shaped walkway over the Grand Canyon. Her vision blurred, and she drew in a deep breath and puffed it out the way the instructor taught her in Lamaze class. If it worked for childbirth, it should work to keep her from passing out now. She forced her gaze down to the glass floor. Thick bands of rust red and tan alternated their way down canyon walls that looked as if they'd been chiseled by a giant sculptor. The shaking in her legs faded. She had to get a picture to take back to her kids.

You can see what's around Linda, and you sense her amazement at the size of the canyon, as well as feel her fear. Emotionally you move with her from fear to wonder to excitement as she thinks about sharing it with her children. We hear it in her thoughts. This is the trick to good internal dialogue. It's what your character is thinking at that moment, the way they would think it. It's like you've planted a listening device in their brain and can play their thoughts on a speaker.

So the next time you're not sure whether you're showing or telling, ask "What would I experience in a holodeck?" That's how you should write it if you want to show rather than tell.

WHAT IS TELLING?

The simple answer would be to say that telling is everything that's not showing, but that's not exact enough for me. What I like to do is compare telling and showing when defining telling.

If showing presents evidence to the reader and allows them to draw their own conclusions, telling dictates a conclusion to the reader, telling them what to believe. It states a fact.

Bob was angry...dictates a conclusion.

But what was the evidence?

Bob punched his fist into the wall.

The Black Plague ravaged the country...dictates a conclusion.

But what was the evidence?

You could describe men loading dead bodies covered in oozing black sores onto a wagon. Your protagonist could press a handkerchief filled with posies to her nose and mouth as she passes someone who's drawing in ragged, labored breaths.

Either of those details, or many others, would show the Black Death ravaging the country.

WHY IS SHOWING NORMALLY BETTER THAN TELLING?

Now that we're clear on the difference between showing and telling, I want to go through why showing is normally better. I think understanding this will help us know when to show and when to tell.

Please notice I said _normally_ better. Later, I'm going to talk about times when telling is actually better than showing.

So normally, showing is better than telling because of the experience it gives to the reader.

Showing respects the reader's intelligence.

Telling assumes that they're not smart enough to understand unless you lay your story out like a lesson plan. We want something explained to us step by step when we're learning a new concept. For example, if you're learning how to solve calculus equations, you want your teacher to tell you how to work through each type of equation. You don't want them to just show you some examples and leave you to work out the bigger principles for yourself. But fiction isn't supposed to be like a lesson in school. Our primary goal isn't to teach—that's what non-fiction books are for.

Showing entertains the reader.

The primary goal of fiction is to entertain. This isn't to say that fiction can't also contain deeper messages. The best fiction does. But it shares those themes through a story. Rather than telling us self-sacrifice is good, it shows us a story of self-sacrifice and allows us to draw our conclusions from that. Think of it this way. If you're a sports fan, what's more entertaining—watching the game yourself or having someone tell you about the game? If you have a favorite TV show, which is more entertaining—watching the show yourself or having someone tell you what happened?

Showing evokes emotion in the reader.

If I told you I was sad, what would you feel? Maybe a little pity for me (if you're a softy). But you're not emotionally invested if I only tell you what I'm feeling. If you see my sadness, watch me struggle with it, and learn the details, suddenly it might touch your heart enough that you find yourself crying along with me. That's what you want your readers to do. That's what showing does. It gives them a vicarious experience.

Showing makes your writing interactive.

From telling stories around the campfire where the story-teller makes the listeners jump to voting for our favorites to win the latest reality TV competition to video games where we create an avatar that looks like us and reacts to our movements, human beings want to interact with what's around them. Showing allows them to do this by actively engaging their minds as they interpret what's happening. And a reader who feels like they're participating in the story is a reader who won't be able to put it down.

In a talk he did for TED, Andrew Stanton, who worked as a writer on movies like *Finding Nemo*, *Toy Story*, and *WALL-E*, pointed out that "the audience actually wants to work for their meal. They just don't want to know that they're doing that. That's your job as a storyteller—to hide the fact that you're making them work for their meal. We're born problem-solvers. We're compelled to deduct and to deduce because that's what we do in real life."

If you'd like to listen to his whole talk, you can find it at the link below.

http://www.ted.com/playlists/62/how_to_tell_a_story.html

This concept of making the audience work a little but keeping it subtle enough that they don't realize that's what's happening is why we need to know when to show (in other words, when to make them work for their meal) and when to tell (keeping it easy enough for them to follow along so that they don't realize they're doing it).

CHAPTER TWO

Techniques to Catch Telling

E ven when we know the difference between showing and telling, and why showing is normally better, telling can be sneaky, so we need some practical ways to identify it. I'm going to take you through eight of the red flags you can search for in your current work-in-progress.

For a lot of these, you'll be able to use the search feature in Microsoft Word (or whatever word processing program you're using) to hunt down words that can indicate telling. For others, you'll have to watch for them as you read through your novel or short story during revisions. I'll talk about that more when we reach the Take It to the Page section later in the book.

Red Flag #1 - Naming Emotions

This is the one we hear about most often, but I want to talk about it anyway because I still see it so frequently in my editing work, and because I don't know where all of you are at on your writing journey.

He was angry. She felt guilty. He hated her.

All of these tell the reader about the emotion rather than showing them. Telling emotion keeps the reader at arm's length rather than letting them experience the emotions along with the character.

Let's take an actual example again.

Telling:

> Jennifer was sad because of the death of her daughter.

Showing:

> Jennifer stood face to face with the delicate porcelain doll Ellie idolized too much to even play with. The doll stared back, her face held in an immortal smile, mocking. No doll deserved to live longer than the little girl who owned her. Jennifer snatched the doll from the shelf and heaved her toward the far wall. The doll's head exploded like a car bomb, fragments flying everywhere.

Most emotions in life are nuanced. Telling allows you to convey only the most basic part of the emotion, whereas showing allows you to bring out all of its facets. In the example above, Jennifer isn't just sad. She's also angry, maybe even a little bitter. That's very different from a character who is sad and guilty, or a character who is sad...but also a little bit relieved. You lose meaning when you tell rather than show emotion.

Showing does force you to do more work in figuring out the layers of emotion your character is feeling, and how to represent those on the page, but the result is well worth it.

A tool I recommend for finding ways to describe emotions (instead of labeling them) is *The Emotion Thesaurus* by Angela Ackerman and Becca Puglisi. If you decide to buy their book, please read Appendix A (How to Make the Best Use of *The Emotion Thesaurus*).

Red Flag #2 - Descriptive Dialogue Tags

When you have a character hiss, growl, beg, demand, or (insert another descriptor here) a sentence, you're violating the *show, don't tell* principle. It's usually a sign of weak dialogue. If you feel like you need to use a tag other than *said*, *asked*, and—occasionally—*whispered* or *shouted* for the reader to understand your meaning, you usually need to rewrite your dialogue and the beats around it to make it stronger and clearer.

Even if you use *asked* or *said*, you might still be telling if you tack on adverbs. (An adverb is a word that modifies a verb, adjective, or another adverb.)

> She said <u>sadly</u>. He asked <u>sulkily</u>. She said <u>angrily</u>.

Time for an example of how we can turn these from telling into showing.

Telling:

> "Are you sure he escaped?" Annabelle asked anxiously.

Showing:

> "What do you mean he *might* have escaped?" Annabelle's gaze darted to the door, and she chewed the edge of her thumb nail. "He either did or he didn't. Which is it?"

Before we move on to the next telling tell, I want to point out that adverbs and adjectives aren't always bad.

To figure out whether an adverb or adjective is worth keeping, ask yourself if the adverb or adjective adds meaning that you can't get in any other way.

Original:

> "You know how he is," she whispered.

With Adverb:

> "You know how he is," she whispered conspiratorially.

But can you see a way to show this?

Showing:

> She brought her hand up beside her mouth as if hiding her words from everyone but me. "You know how he is."

When you want to use an adjective or an adverb, you really need to check that it's giving you a value-add. If it doesn't add value in some way, you need to ask if you're using it as the lazy way out.

Red Flag #3 - Explaining Motivations Using "To"

We each have our private writing demons, and this is mine. If I'm going to fall prey to a telling sin, this will be the one.

Telling:

> She grabbed her bow <u>to shoot the deer</u>. The arrow arced through the air and lodged in the animal's throat. It sank to its knees. Dinner was served.

Most of this is showing. Except for the underlined part. The problem is we don't actually see her shoot. We're told *why* she grabbed her bow, and then the arrow is flying, but we've skipped the part when she fires the shot.

Showing:

> She grabbed her bow, aimed for the deer's heart, and released the string. The arrow arced through the air and lodged in the animal's throat. It sank to its knees. Dinner was served.

I'll give you another example.

Telling:

> Elizabeth went to the woodshed <u>to get the axe</u>. She swung with all her strength and cleaved the stump in two.

First she was going to the woodshed, then she was chopping at the stump, but it feels off because she's jumping locations and we don't see her do it.

Showing:

> Elizabeth went to the woodshed and yanked the axe from where it hung on the wall. She stormed back to the stump, ignoring George's I'd-like-to-see-you-try smirk. She swung with all her strength and cleaved the stump in two. Take that, George. She didn't need any man's help to survive.

You might have noticed that I added internal dialogue to this passage. When you're showing rather than telling, you'll likely have to add additional context to make the meaning of the passage clear and to give the prose a good rhythm.

Red Flag #4 - Helping and State-of-Being Verbs

Helping verbs include *may, might, must, be, being, been, am, are, is, was, were, do, does, did, should, could, would, have, had, has, will, can,* and *shall.*

State-of-being verbs include *is, am, were, was, are, be, being,* and *been.*

We want to avoid these verbs as much as possible in favor of stronger, more active verbs, but we also want to avoid them because they can indicate telling rather than showing.

I'm going to start with an obvious example and move to some that are less obvious.

Telling:

> She <u>was</u> ugly.

Showing:

> Richard couldn't stop himself from staring at the button-sized wart in the middle of her forehead. Even if she didn't want it removed, couldn't she have at least plucked the hair?

One or two carefully selected details will dynamically show us that a person is old or ugly, cruel or a flirt. Moreover, showing also gives us insight into the point-of-view (POV) character. What our characters notice and how they choose to describe it says a lot about them. Richard finds the woman's wart ugly. Another character might not have even noticed it.

Most of you would have probably caught the one I just showed you and known to change it, so I'm going to give you one that might trick a few more of you.

Telling:

> Melanie had trouble breathing.

Or...
Telling:

> Melanie was having trouble breathing.

Here's what most writers are going to do, thinking they've solved the problem.
Attempted Fix:

> Melanie struggled to breathe.

This is still telling. You're reporting a fact, dictating a conclusion, rather than showing the evidence so that the reader can decide what's going on. We don't know what struggling to breathe looks like unless you show us. If you were in a holodeck, how would you experience this?
Showing:

> Melanie bent over, gasping in half-breaths. Blue
> tinged her lips.

Now you can see Melanie and see that she's struggling to breathe. You don't have to be told she is.

Red Flag #5 - *Realized* or *Wondered* as Thoughts

The words *realized* and *wondered* can be an indicator that you're telling the reader the point of view character is realizing or wondering rather than showing them realize or showing them wonder.

Remember this example from when we talked about the holodeck?

Telling:

> Kate realized she'd locked her keys inside the car.

Showing:

> Kate yanked on the car door handle. The door didn't budge, and her keys dangled from the ignition. "Dang it!"

The word *realized* should now be a red flag to you that you might be telling.

Telling:

> She disappeared around the corner. Robert wondered if he'd ever see her again.

Showing:

> She disappeared around the corner. Would he ever see her again?

In the telling version, you the author are telling us what Robert wondered. In the showing version, you're hearing Robert's internal dialogue. In essence, you're showing his thoughts.

There are times when *realized* and *wondered* don't necessarily mean you're telling (usually when you're writing in a first-person POV). Context serves as the deciding factor.

For example...

> I realized I was being difficult, but I didn't care.

If we're in first person point of view, there's no other way the narrator can convey to the reader that they're aware of their actions yet indifferent to any problem those actions might cause.

Other, similar words that could potentially indicate telling and that you should watch for are...

Thought
Knew
Remembered
Recalled
Reviewed
Considered

These won't always indicate telling, but they can. They're all similar in that they're all about what's happening in the character's head, and they all add distance. When in doubt, look at the word in the context of the surrounding passage.

Red Flag #6 - Saw/Smelled/Heard/Felt/Tasted

One thing we need to do to make our fiction come alive is use the five senses. When we first start trying to do that, it's easy to accidentally violate the *show, don't tell* principle through words like *saw, smelled, tasted, felt,* and *heard.* Yet, if we simply do a search for those words and cut them out, we can end up losing important elements of our voice as well.

We need to find the balance. When we do a search for those words in our second (or third or fourth) draft, how can we know when to revise and when to leave them in?

Let's start with a simple example.

Telling:

Pat heard a gunshot in the distance.

Showing:

> A gunshot echoed over the treetops.

In the telling version, we've taken a step back, making ourselves more distant from the story. I'm telling you what happened, but I'm not letting you experience it. In the showing version, we're standing beside Pat (or we're inside his head), and so we experience the sound of the gunshot along with him. This is where point of view and showing vs. telling intersect. If the point-of-view character doesn't experience something, then it can't appear on the page.

In other words, you don't need to tell us he heard a gunshot. Unless Pat is deaf (which could make for an exciting story), we know he heard the gunshot. You need to let us hear the gunshot along with him.

I'll show you another one that uses sight and smell.

Telling:

> Emily saw orange and lemon trees on the horizon line,
> and the air smelled like spoiled fruit.

Not bad, right? You get an idea of where Emily is, and you know it smells bad. But we can bring it alive by bringing it closer.

Showing:

> Orange and lemon trees, limbs sagging with fruit,
> spread out across the length of the horizon. Wafts of fermented citrus made her nose tingle even though she was
> still a quarter mile away.

By taking away *saw* and *smelled*, we're forced to think about vivid details that can bring a scene to life.

This is actually really tricky for writers to master because these terms don't always indicate telling. There are two times in particular when it's okay to use the words *saw, smelled, heard, felt,* or *tasted.*

In Similes

A simile is a figure of speech that compares two unlike things that resemble each other in some way, often using the words *like* or *as.*

I'll give you some examples.

I was in a hospital bed when I regained consciousness. An IV needled poked from the delicate skin on the back of my hand, and I <u>felt</u> like a piece of raw meat pounded flat (from my suspense short story "A Purple Elephant" in *Frozen*).

The healers had smeared Zerynthia's wounds with a fresh coat of green salve so it <u>looked</u> as though she grew moss from her arms and legs. And <u>smelled</u> like rotting leaves in the fall (from my co-written historical fantasy *The Amazon Heir*, releasing in 2015).

His mouth <u>tasted</u> like he'd eaten fresh sewage.

My thoughts <u>felt</u> like a kite caught in a strong wind, tattered and uncontrollable—it was impossible to concentrate.

What I want you to notice is that you need the words *smelled, tasted, looked,* and *felt* in the above examples or you can't write the simile (at least not without replacing them with a boring state-of-being verb like *were* or *was*).

All of these examples could have been written without the simile, and thus kept strictly to showing, but they would have lost their power. I'll show you what I mean. Here's another example. The man has slipped off the edge of a cliff, and the woman is hanging onto his hand, trying to pull him back up.

> He dangled above the hundred-foot drop—the same drop where we'd double bungee jumped a year before and joked about who'd inherit our meager savings if the cord broke. My arm felt like a worn bungee cord now, stretched too thin and ready to snap. I wasn't going to be able to hang on much longer.

This time I'll strip it of the simile to make it strictly show.

> He dangled above the hundred-foot drop—the same drop where we'd double bungee jumped a year before and joked about who'd inherit our meager savings if the cord broke. My shoulder ached, and my arm trembled. I wasn't going to be able to hang on much longer.

There are a lot of other ways that paragraph could have been written, but without the simile, it feels different. You don't get the same visual.

In More Distant POV

If you're writing in omniscient POV or in a very distant third-person POV, then you can include these words because those narrative styles allow it. I'm not saying you *should*. I'm saying you *can*. Technically, omniscient POV is all telling because the narrator isn't a single character. The narrator is someone all-knowing who stands slightly outside of the story.

If you're writing in omniscient POV, make sure you don't use those five-senses words as a crutch. To do omniscient well, you need an even more vibrant voice and an even better eye for key details than when you write in some other POV, because the narrative voice is part of the draw.

Red Flag #7 -
Immediately/Suddenly/Finally

I have a pet peeve about these words. They're telling rather than showing, and 99 times out of 100, if you're doing it right, you don't need them.

So let's dive in starting with *immediately*.

Is there any difference in the meaning of these two passages?

Version 1:

> I punched in the twelve-digit code, and immediately the door swung open.

Version 2:

> I punched in the twelve-digit code. and the door swung open.

Nope. None. Because we don't show a pause or a hesitation, Version 2 shows the reader the exact same thing as Version 1, without the intrusive *immediately*, which is telling the reader what happened rather than allowing them to just watch it play out. It's author intrusion.

Let's look at a similar example involving *suddenly*.

Version 1:

> I leaned against the door and punched the twelve-digit code into the keypad. The door suddenly swung open.

Suddenly is usually added to indicate the character was caught off guard, but it's telling you the character was caught unawares by what happened rather than showing it.

Version 2:

> I leaned against the door and punched the twelve-digit code into the keypad. The door swung open and I fell through, landing on my hands and knees.

We know from the way it's written that the door opened suddenly. We don't need to be told it was sudden.

And finally, we get to *finally*.

Writers often use *finally* as a way to tell us there was a hesitation of some kind, but if the hesitation is important enough to have in the passage, it's probably also important enough to show.

Telling:

> Melody jerked her chin toward Alan. "What do you think?"
>
> Alan hesitated, then finally looked her in the eyes. "We have to at least give him a chance to explain before we kill him."

Showing:

> Melody jerked her chin toward Alan. "What do you think?"
>
> Alan scrubbed a hand through his hair. His gaze moved from the empty jewelry case to Vincent kneeling on the floor, a gun pressed to the back of his head, and returned to her face. "We have to at least give him a chance to explain before we kill him."

Red Flag #8 - Adjective Generalities

Any time you generalize or use an abstraction, you're telling because you're giving the reader a conclusion rather than the evidence. Watch for adjectives—words that modify nouns or pronouns. Adjectives aren't always bad, but they can be a place where generalities slip in.

> An <u>amazing</u> view
> A <u>scary</u> noise
> A <u>big</u> dog

We'll take a longer example.
Telling:

> It was a <u>hot</u> day.

(Notice that this also has the state-of-being verb *was* that we identified earlier as an indicator of telling.)

The problem with generalities is that there's so much room for interpretation. I'm a Canadian. My husband comes from Virginia and did a combat deployment as a Marine to Iraq. What I consider hot and what my husband considers hot aren't the same. How do you see a hot day? What does it feel like? How might you experience it in the holodeck?

Showing:

> Heat radiated off the asphalt in waves, making the world around her ripple. Each puddle she thought she saw disappeared as she approached. She shaded her eyes against the glare. Her forehead was dry to the touch, the sweat that trickled down her temples only minutes before now gone. She should have taken the bottle of water her mom shoved at her. Better yet, she shouldn't

have tried to walk to Jeremy's on a day when even flies refused to come out of the shade and into the sun.

That's a specific kind of hot.

Here's another example.

Telling:

> They walked through the <u>crowded, noisy</u> restaurant.

Showing:

> Randy craned his head above the two couples in front of them. "Doesn't look like we'll get a booth tonight."
> From the far side of the room, rhythmic clapping broke out and a cluster of wait staff launched into a round of "Happy Birthday." Off-key.
> Randy's mouth moved again, and Amy leaned in until her ear bumped his lips. "Say again?"

A crowded, noisy restaurant that's full of children having a birthday party is different from a crowded, noisy restaurant that's full of drunken football fans watching the Super Bowl. Make sure your reader doesn't have to guess which type of noisy and crowded it is.

OBJECTIONS TO SHOWING

Before we move on to talking about the times when we should tell, I want to nail down a couple of the objections I tend to hear about showing rather than telling.

But won't showing make our writing wordy?

You may have noticed that my showing examples were longer than the telling examples we were replacing.

Your showing version will be longer, but that's okay.

Tight writing has less to do with the number of words used and more to do with making every word count.

Make sure the details you pick enhance the story and mean something. Make them reveal character, reflect emotions, foreshadow events, or deepen the theme.

How can I be sure the reader will correctly interpret what I'm trying to show them?

Context.

For example...

> Melody pushed the bowl of soup away.

She might be full, or she might have lost her appetite due to an insult from her boyfriend, or she might find the soup itself unappetizing because of the look or smell. It's the context that will make it clear to the reader.

> Melody sniffed the steaming bowl, wrinkled her nose, and pushed it away.

The reader will know Melody doesn't like the way the soup smells and thus doesn't want to eat it. You don't need to say "Melody didn't like the way the soup smelled" or "Melody found the soup too stinky to eat."

Now that we've looked at ways to catch telling and destroy it, I want to move on to looking at times when we should actually be telling rather than showing in our writing.

CHAPTER THREE

Telling as a First Draft Tool

I know this is going to sound strange to those of you who write a slow but beautiful first draft, but the drafting stage is one time where you might be better off telling rather than slowing down to figure out how to show. Then, during your revision stage, you can work on replacing your telling with showing. (And the more we grow as writers, the less telling we're likely to find in our first drafts.)

Using telling as a first draft tool is advice I might not have given a few years ago. I used to have a reputation for writing painstakingly slow first drafts that were ready to go. I'm serious. Some of the work I'm most proud of is work that went from first draft to submitted and won awards. But I wrote at the speed of someone trying to catch soap bubbles from the air without popping them.

The problem with this was a problem I think many writers experience. There's a lot of pressure, and it's easy to become discouraged and go for days or weeks without writing a single word. It's hard to motivate yourself to devote two hours to writing knowing you might only come out with 250 new words.

At the start of 2013, I went on a quest to find ways to increase my word count. One step along that path was taking Rachel Funk Heller's *Writing the Emotion Draft* class. The idea behind this class is to write an entire novel in two weeks. You know the book will need revision after, but the idea is that the emotion will be on the page due to freeing your mind from over-analyzing as you write.

I learned a lot from pushing myself to write faster, and one of the key tricks I discovered was the power of using telling as a stand in. If I'd slowed down every time I needed to pick the right details to show, I wouldn't have been able to go from writing 250 words an hour to 2000 words an hour.

I used telling as a placeholder to get down the general idea I was aiming for, knowing I could pick the perfect details to express that concept during revision.

I wrote faster and felt excited about writing again.

Here's my caveat to this advice: If you're the kind of writer whose words solidify once they hit the page, and you have a difficult time changing them during revisions, don't do this.

If you're a writer who is open to adding the details later, this is a great way to not only increase your productivity but also have more fun writing again.

(If you'd like to read more about the tricks I discovered for increasing my writing speed, take a look at my mini-book, *How to Write Faster.*)

CHAPTER FOUR

When Should We Tell Rather than Show in a Finished Manuscript?

Times do exist when it's better to tell than to show, even in a finished manuscript. In 2011, I had the privilege of being mentored by Randy Ingermanson (of Snowflake Method and Advanced Writing E-Zine fame) at a conference. One of the things I remember best is what he said about showing and telling—it's all about balance.

In the situations I'm going to walk you through next, telling is actually better than showing.

When You're Dealing with an Insignificant Fact

When he needs to decide whether to show or tell, award-winning science fiction writer Robert J. Sawyer asks, "Will it be on the test?" In other words, when you take the time to show something, readers assume it's important to the story. If you spend two paragraphs showing the snow and ice, later in the story you'd better have someone's car slide off the road or someone near death from hypothermia. Or you need to use it to reveal something about the character or their emotions. Otherwise, just tell the reader "It was snowing, and ice covered the roads."

I found a great example of this in K.M. Wieland's *Dreamlander*. In the passage I'm going to show you, the main character, Chris, has just watched someone get shot. The author shows us the shooting in a scene, but what I want you to see is how she moves from showing to telling and back to showing again because I'm going to talk about why she does it this way.

I've put the showing in bold and the telling in italics, and I've underlined her transitions.

He called 911, pinned the phone against his shoulder, and used both hands to rip open Harrison's thin undershirt.

He'd gotten himself into a whole lot more than he's bargained for right here.

***

Ten minutes later, a police car, followed by an ambulance, arrived. After another half an hour, the detective finally got around to talking to Chris. Nobody seemed to know anything about what had happened. At any rate, not anything they wanted to tell him.

It was a whole hour more before they let him walk back up the street to where he'd parked the Bug. <u>He had the key in the lock, turning it, when a footstep sounded behind him.</u>

"Hey," someone said.

He turned to look, and something hard smashed into the back of his head.

So you can see that she's drawing to the end of the actual scene and uses a scene break (the three asterisks in green/underlined), then when she starts up again, we're in telling mode.

When we hit the second patch of green/underlining, she's blending showing and telling in a way that signals a transition is about to happen from the telling she's been doing into showing again.

Now, the important question for us is why she chooses to tell in the passage above.

At first glance, if you're still learning when to show and when to tell, it might look like she should have played this out in a scene. Wouldn't it have been exciting to see the police interrogate Chris? While they're interrogating him, he could be trying to get information from them as well. She could have written it so that they suspected him and created a tense, conflict-filled scene.

But she didn't, and she didn't for a very good reason. No matter how exciting she might have been able to make that interrogation/questioning scene, it didn't matter to the story overall. She showed the important parts, which were Harrison getting shot and then Chris getting hit in the head, but she told the part in the middle in order to condense time when the details didn't matter to the story. They weren't going to be on the test.

But that raises another question. If they're not essential to the story, why include them at all?

In this case, we need them for the story to make sense. If she didn't tell us that the emergency personnel came and talked to Chris and then finally let him go, we, as readers, would be wondering about what happened after Chris called

911. So we need to have it in there for the story to work, but it's insignificant, so we don't need to spend the time on showing it.

During Transitions

This is a similar situation. Sometimes you just need to get a character from point A to point B without bringing the story to a grinding halt by describing it.

> The next morning, Marilyn drove to Bob's house.

We don't need to see Marilyn drive to Bob's house. We just need to know she did. We don't need you to describe the sunrise or the morning traffic jam in detail to try to get around telling us she went in the morning.

Here's another example.

> Half an hour later, they arrived at the mountain summit.

If nothing eventful happened on the climb, if it wasn't essential to the story for us to see them climbing, we don't need the blow by blow.

Sometimes, narrative is the best, most efficient way to get the job done.

When You Need to Compress Time or Set-Up an Important Scene

Sometimes in a story you'll have a situation where you want to let the reader know something has happened multiple times, but to actually show it happening multiple times would destroy the pace of the story. Or perhaps you need the reader to know very early in the book (prior to the inciting incident that kicks off your whole plot) that something has been happening repeatedly, and you don't have the luxury of 50–100 pages where you can casually drop in mentions of the repeated event.

In those cases, you're best to use telling to condense time so you can move on to what's truly important to the story (and will be more interesting for the reader).

For example, let's say we're writing a historical novel about a woman dealing with abandonment by her husband in a time period when women needed the financial support and protection of a man to survive. As the book opens, he's filled her head with dreams of a better life out west. He empties their bank account. He's going to go ahead of her and send her a letter with instructions on how to join him as soon as he's there and settled.

> Each day I walked to the post office to check our box. Each day the clerk came back empty-handed. At first it was, "Is there something special coming, dear?" and then "Are you sure he has the right address?" and finally "Letters get lost all the time. I wouldn't worry." By the time winter set in, she didn't say anything at all. When I asked if I had any mail, she simply shook her head. She wouldn't look me in the eyes.

Since the conflict of the book is this woman's survival post-abandonment, we don't want to spend pages and pages establishing the fact that, for whatever reason, her husband isn't going to send for her. We don't want to have to show her repeatedly going to the post office, looking for a letter. We want to condense this time in her life to get the important information across and move on to the real focus of the story.

Helen Fielding uses this technique in *Bridget Jones's Diary* when Bridget recounts how, every time her mother has called her in weeks, she's mentioned Mark Darcy. Fielding did it in two quick paragraphs where she recounted the snippet of each conversation where Bridget's mom (not so subtly) brought up Mark Darcy, and it sets up the all-important scene where Bridget and Mark meet for the first time.

(You can take a peek at it using the preview feature at any online retailer. It happens in Chapter Two, under the 11.45 pm heading.)

Fielding could have shown us a scene where Bridget was on the phone with her mom, and she could have used internal dialogue to indicate that this wasn't the first time her mom brought up Mark Darcy. But to do that, she would have needed to include a lot of unnecessary words to set up the conversation and lead into the important element, which was her mother desperately wanting her to hook up with Mark Darcy, and Bridget just as desperately not wanting to have anything to do with him.

Writing these types of situations as scenes wouldn't be wrong because we do need to build anticipation in the reader before the "main event" happens, but it's alright to make a stylistic choice to compress time and set up the scene using telling. It's tricky to do this well, but when it works, it can be great.

When Showing Would Bog Down Your Story or Confuse Your Reader

Sometimes the reader absolutely needs to know a fact that all the characters already know, and creating a scene to show that fact is going to slow down the story and feel forced. Telling the information is a much better solution in this situation than using something like As-You-Know-Bob dialogue, which always feels unnatural and awkward. (I've added an explanation of As-You-Know-Bob dialogue in Appendix B.)

This need to tell most commonly happens with backstory and technical information. If the characters share a common history or common profession, or are working together on the same goal or project, they'll often already know the key pieces of information your reader needs.

In Kim Stanley Robinson's *Red Mars*, the first in his series about the colonization of Mars, the plot depends on complex technological and biochemical ideas. Robinson can't stop and create a scene every time he needs to give the reader a piece of information. The story would be unreasonably long and slow. He also can't leave it out or the story wouldn't make sense to readers. He instead chooses to feed it to the reader's in small bites of telling.

Another writer who routinely did this well was Michael Crichton. If you've ever read *Jurassic Park*, you'll remember that he gives you a lot of technical information, but he does it in such a way that you don't mind.

Here's an example from my science fiction short story, "Echolocation." The story opens as the leaders of the main character's world are deciding whether to abandon their planet or continue their seemingly futile attempts to kill the king of the alien race they're at war with. It's essential to the plot of the story that the reader know why these two races are at war, why peace is impossible, and why their only options are to win or abandon their planet. Leaving out this information would leave the reader confused. However, everyone in the story knows the history between the two races. And because of where the story starts, there's no way to introduce that backstory in a scene without it feeling unnatural or slowing the story down to a crawl.

The best solution was to drop in a single telling paragraph and move on with the plot.

When they'd taken pity on the homeless Balati and let them move from their armada of ships to the planet's surface, they hadn't known the reason no other society would take them in was that they excreted an airborne toxin from their skin. Prolonged exposure acted like a virus, attacking the victim's retinas. By the time they figured it out, the Balati were already established on the surface and refused to leave.

You might want to argue that we should leave the history a mystery for the readers to discover as they go along. In many cases, you do want to hold information back because withholding information creates some of the tension in any story. A good story should have some secrets.

At the same time, you have to decide where you want the reader's focus to be. Do you want them working to piece together backstory? Or do you want them working alongside your protagonist to figure out who the killer is, or why the town's water supply has turned red like blood, or where the treasure is hidden, or how your main character can make it home alive?

This is an important distinction to make. We want the reader to be engaged but not confused. If they need the backstory or technical information to understand the story, just give it to them. Sometimes it's better to give them the backstory or technical information they need rather than leaving them to puzzle it out for themselves, because that frees them up to be engaged with the important elements of the story happening in the present.

When you're telling in a situation like this, make sure you do it in small bites and that you make it interesting. You also want to try to do it at a time when it would feel natural for the point-of-view character to be thinking about the information.

When you're deciding whether or not to set up an entire scene or to use some other device (e.g., introducing a character who doesn't know the fact, solely for the purpose of conveying it to the reader), the question you need to ask yourself is *how important is this to the story?*

The more important it is to the story, the more likely it is that you should take the time to create a scene around it. The less important it is to the story, the more likely it is you should slip the information in as quickly and unobtrusively as possible. If you have a lot of information that needs to be delivered quickly, it's okay to tell it rather than showing it and risking bringing the story to a grinding halt.

If you'd like other examples of effective telling to convey information, take a look at "20 Great Infodumps from Science Fiction Novels" on io9.com.

When Showing Would Bore Your Reader

Sometimes a reader has already seen a scene play out (you've shown it), but the character who was involved needs to catch up other characters. Showing it again through a dialogue play-by-play would put the reader to sleep.

For example, let's say Barry had a huge fight with his wife because she admitted she's pregnant and doesn't know who the father is. Could be Barry. Could be the man she's been having an affair with for six months. You write an amazing scene, and then Barry storms off to his brother's house.

Barry needs to tell his brother what just happened, but the reader doesn't need to sit through it all again. You can use indirect dialogue instead.

Barry filled Frank in on what had happened.

"What am I going to do?"

The bolded indirect dialogue is telling.

When You're Going to Interpret It to Add Emotional Punch

Sometimes, when done with a light hand, you can combine telling and showing to create a more powerful emotional punch than either could give on their own.

I'll give you an example to show you what I mean.

> His hands shook so slightly I wouldn't have noticed it had he not picked up the teacup. Just a ripple on the surface of the liquid. The clink of the china bumping his top teeth. My throat closed, and I couldn't choke down what remained in my own cup. He was afraid. I'd never seen my husband afraid before, not in all our ten years of marriage, not in all the times we'd traveled to hostile locations, not even when he caught malaria and almost died that month we spent in Africa.

In this example, we have the show of his hands shaking, and we see the narrator (his wife) react to it. That would have been fine had it ended there. But because the narrator labels his emotion and then interprets it for us, we get an added emotional punch. Fear isn't normal for this man. He doesn't seem to fear dying. So what could shake him so badly?

The key to making telling work in this type of situation is to only use it when you're going to have the point-of-view character interpret the situation. The example above would have been the bad kind of telling had it read something like...

> His hands shook slightly in fear, and my throat closed. I couldn't choke down what remained in my own cup.

No interpretation. It tells when we've already shown without giving the tell a good reason to be there. If you're going to add a tell to something you've already shown, you need to be certain it's giving you something powerful in exchange for the space it's taking up.

In Your Opening Sentence

This might sound crazy at first, but look at a lot of the strong first lines from all genres of novels. You'll see what could be considered telling. (Personally, I prefer to call it *compelling narrative*.)

> I was thirteen when I found out why my mother left me. – from *Red* by Kait Nolan.

> Kaduis couldn't take pleasure in having women thrown at his feet. Not this day. – from *The Amazon Heir* by Marcy Kennedy and Lisa Hall-Wilson (releasing 2015)

> You get yourself into strange places when you're broke, jobless, and trying to figure out how to pay back sixty thousand dollars in college loans. Such as dark,

musty mine shafts that have been abandoned for a hundred years – from *Torrent* by Lindsay Buroker

Keryn Wills was in the shower when she decided how to kill Josh Trenton. – from *Double Vision* by Randy Ingermanson

If you want more examples, check out *Transgression* by Randy Ingermanson, *Gone Girl* by Gillian Flynn, *The Forgotten* by David Baldacci, *The Sweet Spot* by Laura Drake, *The Light Between Oceans* by M. L. Stedman, or *The Language of Flowers* by Vanessa Diffenbaugh. All of their first lines are telling.

The trick to using telling in the first line of your story is to make sure it encourages the reader to ask the question "Why?"

Why did the narrator's mother leave when the narrator was thirteen? (in *Red*)

Why couldn't Kaduis take pleasure in having women thrown at his feet on this particular day? (in *The Amazon Heir*)

Why is the narrator down in a dusty mine shaft? (in *Torrent*)

Why does Keryn need to kill Josh? (in *Double Vision*)

Why does he always think of his wife's head when he thinks of his wife? (in *Gone Girl*)

Why is he afraid that tonight is going to be his last night on earth? (in *The Forgotten*)

Why was she thankful for bull semen? (in *The Sweet Spot*)

Why did the narrator dream of fire? (in *The Language of Flowers*)

These telling examples all work because they make the reader ask a question. Wanting to know the answer to that question is what motivates them to read on.

Telling isn't always bad.

The trick with writing is that we have to learn the guidelines before we can know when to break them, and when we break them, we have to be sure we're breaking them because it makes the story better rather than because we want to be rebels, because we're lazy, or because we think the rules don't apply to us. The rules do apply to us, lazy writing is crappy writing, and there's no value in being a rebel just for the sake of it.

CHAPTER FIVE

Take It to the Page Practical Applications

I f you're working on your first draft, or if you're reading this book to get a working knowledge of the topic but aren't ready yet to work on revising/editing your book based on what you're learning, skip this section for now. When you're ready to start rewrites/edits, you can always come back to it then.

In many of my books, the Take It to the Page sections appear at the end of the individual chapters. In this case, I felt it was important for you to have the full picture of when to show and when to tell before you started working on revisions. Otherwise, you might have changed telling to showing when it should have stayed as it was. For that reason, I've turned this book's Take It to the Page into a chapter of its own. The revision items are still broken down for you by which chapter the concepts were first presented in.

Chapter One

Chapter One's Take It to the Page section is meant to help you become more comfortable with recognizing showing and telling. The following Take It to the Page sections will focus on identifying specific types of showing and telling and fixing them when needed.

Step 1 – Choose a chapter from your current manuscript.

Step 2 – Using either the highlighter tool in your word processing program or a highlighter and a paper printout, highlight any passages that you think might be telling, or that you aren't sure whether they're showing or telling.

Step 3 – For each highlighted section, ask yourself, "If this were a holodeck program, would I be able to experience this?" If the answer is *yes*, move on to the next highlighted passage in your book. If the answer is *no*, move on to Step 4.

Step 4 – If you couldn't experience this passage in a holodeck, then you've dictated a conclusion to the reader. Jot down three examples of evidence that would help the reader decide for themselves. Trying to think of three instead of just one when we're first learning to switch from showing to telling helps us find a fresh way to show.

Chapter Two

In Chapter Two's Take It To The Page section, you're going to depend heavily on the Find or Search feature in your word processing program. However, if you prefer, you can manually take it to the page by reading through each chapter multiple times, working on one or two steps with each pass. Going manually takes longer, but will help you internalize the concepts better. This means you'll likely find less telling and more showing in your future projects. Using your word processing program's Find feature will be quicker and easier. This is a trade-off, and only you can decide which method is best for you and for the needs of your current story.

Step 1 – Run a search for the emotion-themed words in the following list. These are by no means the only words for emotions, but they'll help you catch the most common ones. (You might also want to try variations on the word or try typing in the root of the word—for example, type in *sad*, not *sadness*, because a search for *sad* will show you *sad, sadness, sadly*, etc.) Are you naming the emotion the character is feeling? Figure out your character's root emotion, the nuances of it, and why they're feeling it, and then create a fresh way to show that emotion to the reader.

afraid
agitated
alarmed
amazed
ambivalent
amused
angry
anguish
annoyed
anxious
aroused
ashamed
bitter
bored

calm
cautious
cheerful
comfortable
compassion
concerned
confident
conflicted
confused
contempt
content
curious
defeated
defensive
delighted
depressed
desperate
determined
disappointed
disgusted
disillusioned
dismayed
disoriented
distrust
doubtful
dread
eager
elated
embarrassed
enthusiastic
envious

excited
exhausted
fond
frustrated
grateful
grief
grumpy
guilty
happy
hateful
helpless
hesitant
hopeful/hopeless
horrified
hostile
humiliated
hurt
impatient
indifferent
infatuated
inferior
insecure
insulted
interested
intrigued
irritated
isolated
jealous
joyful
lonely
mad

nervous
nostalgic
numb
optimistic
outraged
overwhelmed
panic
paranoid
pity
proud
rage
regretful
rejected
relaxed
relieved
reluctant
remorseful
resentful
resigned
restless
revulsion
sad
safe
satisfied
scornful
self-conscious
shame
shocked
skeptical
smug
sorrowful

spiteful
stressed
stunned
surprised
suspicious
sympathetic
tired
uncomfortable
vengeful
wary
weary
worried

Step 2 – Search for the dialogue tag words in the following list. Are you telling rather than showing? Do you absolutely need these words to get your meaning across, or is there another way you could show the meaning? Rewrite so that you only need to use *said, asked, whispered, yelled,* or the adverb examples discussed in this chapter.

acknowledged
admitted
agreed
angled
answered
argued
babbled
barked
begged
bellowed
bemoaned

blurted
blustered
bragged
breathed
commented
complained
confessed
cried
croaked
crooned
crowed
demanded
denied
drawled
echoed
faltered
fumed
giggled
groaned
growled
grumbled
heckled
hinted
hissed
howled
implored
inquired
inserted
interjected
interrupted
jested

laughed
mumbled
murmured
muttered
nagged
offered
opined
orated
pleaded
pouted
promised
queried
questioned
quipped
quoted
raged
ranted
reiterated
remembered
replied
requested
retorted
roared
ruminated
sang
scolded
screamed
screeched
shouted
shrieked
sighed

snarled

snickered

snorted

sobbed

sputtered

stammered

stuttered

threatened

thundered

told

wailed

warned

whimpered

whined

wondered

yelped

Step 3 – Search for the words *asked, said, whispered, shouted,* and *yelled.* (These are also called dialogue tags.) Each time you find one, ask yourself these questions.

- ✓ Does your dialogue tag have an adverb attached to it?
- ✓ Does the adverb indicate something you couldn't convey through either a stronger verb or stronger dialogue? If not, rewrite your dialogue and beats so that you can delete the adverb.

Step 4 – Explaining motivations using the word *to* is one of the more difficult instances of telling to catch because there's no easy way to use the Search or Find features of your word processing program. Read through the chapter you're working on and look specifically for instances where your character does one thing <u>to</u> do something else. (E.g., "She grabbed her bow <u>to</u> shoot the deer.") Change each of these spots so that your character performs the two actions. (E.g., "She grabbed her bow <u>and</u> shot the deer.")

Step 5 – You can do this step in two different ways depending on your word processing program and how you prefer to work. We're going to be looking for helping and state-of-being verbs.

Option A

If you have a word processing program (like Microsoft Word 2010 or newer) that will highlight every instance of a word that you search for, run a search for the words *is, was,* and *were.* For each result, ask yourself the following questions.

- ✓ Am I reporting a fact? (E.g., "She was ugly.") If so, how could I give evidence instead?
- ✓ What carefully selected details would best lead readers to the correct conclusion?
- ✓ Is the detail I've chosen to use consistent with what my point-of-view character would notice?
- ✓ Can the helping or state-of-being verbs you've located be removed to make your writing tighter and stronger?

Helping and state-of-being verbs can often be replaced by stronger, tighter verbs. For example...

Emily was walking to work.

Becomes...

> Emily walked to work.

Option B

If you prefer to do this step by hand, print out a chapter of your book. Use a fresh highlighter color and highlight all of the helping or state-of-being verbs listed in this chapter.

Is your page littered with highlights? This can be an indication not only of telling, but also that you need to work on replacing helping or state-of-being verbs with stronger, tighter verbs.

For example...

> Emily was walking to work.

Becomes...

> Emily walked to work.

Can the helping or state-of-being verbs you've located be removed to make your writing tighter and stronger?

For the rest, are you reporting a fact? (E.g., "She was ugly.") If so, how can you give evidence instead? What carefully selected details would best lead readers to the correct conclusion? Is the detail you've chosen to use consistent with what your point-of-view character would notice?

Step 6 – Search for the words in the following list. Have you used these words to tell the reader that your point-of-view character is thinking, rather than just showing *what* the character is thinking?

realized

wondered

thought

knew

remembered

recalled

reviewed

considered

Step 7 – If you're writing in omniscient POV, consider skipping this step.

Do a search for the words *saw, smelled, tasted,* and *heard.* (If you're writing in present tense, you'll need to change the tense to match.) Have you used these words as part of a simile or to try to describe one of the five senses? If they're part of a simile, move on to the next one. If you've used them to try to describe one of the five senses, can you make it more vivid and immediate by rewriting the sentence without *saw, smelled, tasted,* or *heard?*

Step 8 – Do a search for the word *felt.* (If you're writing in present tense, you'll need to change the tense to match.)

Have you used *felt* as part of a simile or to try to describe one of the five senses? If you've used it as part of a simile, move on to the next one. If you've used it to try to describe one of the five senses, can you make it more vivid and immediate by rewriting the sentence without *felt?*

Have you used this word to name an emotion? (E.g., "She felt sad over the death of her daughter.") This will help you catch any instances of naming emotions that you might have missed in Step 1. Figure out what your character is feeling (and why), and then create a fresh way to show that emotion to the reader.

Step 9 – Do a search for the words *immediately, suddenly,* and *finally.* Does the sentence need this word for the meaning to be clear? Does it add anything to the meaning of the sentence? Can you rewrite the sentence (and perhaps the ones around it) to better show what these words are telling?

Step 10 – Do a search for the word *hesitated.* Is the fact that the character hesitated important enough to point it out? If it is, find a way to rewrite the passage to show the character hesitating.

Step 11 – Go through each chapter and read the passages where you've described something. Highlight any adjectives—words that modify nouns or pronouns. Examples of adjectives include *amazing, scary, big,* and *hot.* Have you generalized in your description? Can you make your description more specific to give the reader a clearer picture?

Step 12 – When you finish analyzing a chapter for showing and telling, check your showing passages. Is your intended meaning clear? If not, what context do you need to add to make it clearer for the reader?

Chapter Four

In Chapter Four's Take It to the Page section, you'll be stepping back from the Find feature of your word processing program and mainly looking at the bigger picture of your book.

Step 1 – Don't read through each of your scenes. Instead, think of them on a big-picture scale. Is everything that you've shown in this scene important to the overall story? Do you have any rabbit trail scenes that might be exciting when taken individually but don't contribute enough to the story as a whole to justify their existence? Part of balancing showing and telling is knowing when to tell something because it's not significant to the plot.

Step 2 – Skim your book, looking for transitions. Have you tried to show them, slowing down the pace? If they're only included because a character needs to get from point A to point B, consider telling them instead of showing them.

Step 3 – Does your book have a situation where you want to let the reader know that something has happened multiple times, but to actually show it happening multiple times would destroy the pace of the story? Or do you need the reader to know very early in the book (prior to the inciting incident that kicks off your whole plot) that something has been happening repeatedly? Consider how you could compress time to tell this. Make sure you tell in an interesting way.

Step 4 – Skim your book for spots where you've tried to convey information that your characters already know (backstory or technical information) to the reader. Have you fallen prey to As-You-Know-Bob Syndrome in your dialogue? If so, find a spot where your point-of-view character would naturally be thinking about the information. Insert it quickly, using telling in no more than three or four sentences.

Step 5 – Skim your book, looking for scenes where one character is telling another character something the reader has already seen happen. Consider using a line or two of indirect dialogue instead.

Step 6 – Find three or four spots where you want to add an extra emotional punch. Can you tell an emotion and interpret it for the reader?

Step 7 – Read the first line of your story. Have you shown or told? Could you write a telling first line that would be more powerful than a showing first line? Remember that the key to using telling in the first line of your story is to make sure it encourages the reader to ask the question "Why?"

For a printable version of the Take It to the Page section and clickable links for all of the external resources I recommended in this book, go to www.marcykennedy.com/showtell.

Password: iseeit

How to Make the Best Use of *The Emotion Thesaurus*

A s writers, our job is to create a meaningful emotional experience for readers. One of the best ways to do this is to convey
the quality and depth of our characters' feelings through their
thoughts, body language, and visceral reactions. This is the primary
focus of The Emotion Thesaurus: A Writer's Guide to Character Expression and is at the root of the "show, don't tell" principle.

– Angela Ackerman & Becca Puglisi in *Emotion Amplifiers*
(A Companion Guide to *The Emotion Thesaurus*)

Writers are just like every other profession in one important way—the right tools make our job easier.

The Emotion Thesaurus is one of those tools.

When we're writing, it's easy to fall into certain standbys
without even realizing it. He's angry—he frowns. She's frustrated—she sighs.

But those unimaginative responses don't begin to do credit to the variety of non-verbal communication we use every day or to the unique, three-dimensional characters we're supposed to create.

That's where *The Emotion Thesaurus* comes in, and I wanted to give you the three ways I think *The Emotion Thesaurus* can help you write better stories.

(Just for the record – I don't get any sort of compensation if you buy *The Emotion Thesaurus*. I'm recommending it because I've used it, liked it, and think it can be a valuable tool.)

The Emotion Thesaurus Saves Research Time

Because I want to find fresh ways to express emotions in my writing, I often spend a lot of time, especially at the editing stage, looking up emotions online and studying non-verbal communication. Even as someone who has a degree in social psychology and loves digging into what makes people tick, I don't enjoy how much time this eats up, and I'm tempted to skip it.

The Emotion Thesaurus brings the research you need together in one place. Each entry defines the emotion and gives physical signals, internal sensations, mental responses, signs of that emotion over the long term, and cues that the emotion is being repressed.

What that allows us to do is figure out what emotion our character is feeling and look through the lists to find expressions that fit our character and the situation they're in.

Then we can personalize it. For example, one of the internal sensations for agitation is feeling overheated. How will your character describe that sensation? A middle-aged woman with a good sense of humor might think of it in terms of getting a taste of the hot flashes she'll experience in menopause. A teenager might liken it to when the air conditioning broke in their house for three whole days. A character with money might describe it as similar to how he felt when he stayed in the sauna too long. Same sensation. Different points of view. Infinite possibilities.

The Emotion Thesaurus Helps with Ideas for Increasing Tension

As you read through the list of characteristics for the emotion you want to convey, you'll notice that some symptoms of that emotion are perfect for increasing tension.

In the agitation entry, the first three mental responses listed are

- mounting frustration that causes thoughts to blank,
- compounding mistakes, and
- a tendency to lie to cover up or excuse.

You can use agitation to lay the groundwork for bad things to come or to make the current scene more stressful. Many emotions, even positive ones, can have these undesirable consequences.

Becca and Angela also include a "Writer's Tip" at the end of each emotion with a special hint for other ways you can use that particular emotion to add tension or some other depth to your story.

The Emotion Thesaurus Keeps Characters' Emotional Arcs Believable

One of the tricks Blake Snyder shares in *Save the Cat* is that, in every scene, the character needs to end at a different emotional place than where they began. I struggle with this because I tend to be hyper-logical and tamp down on my emotions. I'm not always certain of the progression an emotion might take in someone who's less like a Borg.

Becca and Angela added a "May Escalate To" list for each emotion. So, for example, if your character starts the scene agitated (or becomes agitated early on in the scene), you can look at the list and see that likely emotional outcomes by the end of the scene or in the following scene are annoyance, frustration, anxiety, or anger. Then you can go look at the physical signs of those emotions. It helps us bring our character to that next step.

Another thing mentioned by Becca and Angela in their front matter (which is a great look at emotion in itself) is that we often need to seek the root emotion to bring out the correct signs. A person might believe they're angry, but that anger might actually be a cover-up for something else. So while your character might be screaming at their teenager for wrecking the car, they're also grabbing their child into a hug because the true emotion isn't anger—it's fear and relief that their child survived.

Dissecting an Example

I f you're confident that you understand showing and telling by this point, you don't need to read this appendix. However, many of us learn better by seeing concepts applied. That's the purpose of this section. I'm going to give you a sample passage full of writing craft errors. I won't be addressing every error in the example, but I am going to pull it apart to show you how to solve the showing-telling problems and how to do a little bit of tightening. Because showing will add more words, we want to make sure that every word counts.

Here we go...

> Trying her best to wrestle her way into her too-tight coat, Vanessa blurted out, "We're going to be late if you don't hurry up."
>
> Edward glanced up from the papers scattered around him on the floor. "Sure thing," he mumbled.
>
> Becoming upset, she repeated, "We're going to be late. Do you even know what time it is?"

Edward reached for the clock sitting on the small end table beside the couch. It read 4:45. "It's only a fifteen-minute drive. We don't need to leave for another half hour yet."

"Our appointment's at five," she said, an annoyed and anxious expression on her face.

"What?" he asked as he struggled to get up without scattering his work. Grumbling, he said, "Why didn't you tell me sooner?"

"I reminded you an hour ago," her voice reached a new tone. "If we lose our chance at adopting a baby..."

Her words hit him like a slap in the face. "I'm ready," he said, rushing to get dressed and running a comb through his knotted hair. "We can still make it on time."

Now it's time to break the example down and pull out the errors. I'll repeat the sentence we're going to look at, with the important part bolded.

Trying her best to wrestle her way into her too-tight coat, Vanessa blurted out, "We're going to be late if   . you don't hurry up."

What does that trying look like? I run into this a lot in the fiction I edit where people try to wave or try to stand up, and it's telling because you don't leave the reader with a clear picture of what's happening. Did they actually wave or stand, or didn't they?

Although the point-of-view character isn't clear at the start of this passage (another error), it's Edward, which means how he describes Vanessa's wrestle with her coat will also tell us something about him. Does he describe her as looking like a child who doesn't know how to dress herself? (This option suggests he feels like he always needs to take care of her.) Or like a circus clown making a big production to get a reaction from the crowd? (This option suggests he thinks she's making a bigger deal out of her coat than it needs to be just so that he'll pay attention to her.)

A similar situation happens again a few paragraphs later.

> "What?" he asked **as he struggled to get up without scattering his work.** Grumbling, he said, "Why didn't you tell me sooner?"

What does struggling to get up without scattering his work look like? Does he pick his way around the piles on tiptoes? Does he climb over the back of the couch?

As we move on, we have more than one instance of creative dialogue tags.

> Trying her best to wrestle her way into her too-tight coat, Vanessa **blurted** out, "We're going to be late if you don't hurry up."
>
> Edward glanced up from the papers scattered around him on the floor. "Sure thing," he **mumbled.**
>
> Becoming upset, she **repeated,** "We're going to be late. Do you even know what time it is?"

But there's something else I want to show you that's happening. Throughout this passage, tags and beats have been used to identify who's speaking the dialogue. A *tag* is a word like *said* or *asked*. A *beat* is a piece of action. You usually only need one, and this is a great way to tighten up your writing.

> Trying her best to wrestle her way into her too-tight coat, Vanessa **blurted** out, "We're going to be late if you don't hurry up."

Becomes...

> Vanessa wrestled her way into her too-tight coat. "We're going to be late if you don't hurry up."

Occasionally you'll use a tag and a beat, but when you do, it needs to be an intentional move on your part for the sake of rhythm. (If you're interested in learning more about dialogue, check out my *How to Write Dialogue: A Busy Writer's Guide*.)

Going back to the main passage, we run into spots where we have named emotions.

> **Becoming upset**, she repeated, "We're going to be late. Do you even know what time it is?"

Think about it this way. How many of us are really good at identifying and naming our own emotions (the real root emotion)? If we're an introspective type of person, we might analyze and name our emotions in hindsight, but how many of us do it at the time? We don't. We feel the emotions rather than naming them. That's what your characters should do, too, especially in times of high emotion.

> "Our appointment's at five," she said, an **annoyed and anxious expression** on her face.

What does an annoyed and anxious expression look like? More specifically, what does Vanessa, this particular character, look like when she's annoyed and anxious?

The next part I want you to look at demonstrates an important principle.

Edward **reached for the clock** sitting on the small
end table beside the couch. It read 4:45. "It's only a fifteen-minute drive. We don't need to leave for another
half hour yet."

This is the same concept as what we talked about in the
section on explaining motivations using "to," such as "She
drew her bow to shoot the deer."

Rather than seeing Edward reaching, we should see him
grab. The reaching is implied in a way the grabbing isn't because, to grab, it's a necessity that you also had to reach. If you
reach, it's not a necessity that you also have to grab.

As we move further into the passage, we run into a sneaki-
er form of telling.

"I reminded you an hour ago," her voice **reached a
new tone**. "If we lose our chance at adopting a baby..."

What changes in her tone? You're back in the holodeck
now. How do you experience this? A change in tone could
mean a lot of things, and we can't hear it unless the author
plays the sound track for us.

Here's the last bit I'm going to pull out today.

Her words hit him like a slap in the face. "I'm ready,"
he said, rushing to get dressed and running a comb
through his **knotted** hair. "We can still make it on
time."

I wanted to pull this particular part out to show you how
what's showing and what's telling sometimes depends on who
the point-of-view character is.

Sometimes we could get away with that description. For example, if Vanessa were the POV character and she's thinking about his knotted hair and how she hopes he brushes it before they go to the meeting, then it would be okay for her to think about his hair as knotted.

But because we're in Edward's point of view, this is telling. If we're in Edward's body, since he's the POV character, it should go more like this...

> Her words hit him like a slap in the face. "I'm ready." He pulled yesterday's pants off the back of the chair and hopped on one leg while sliding the other in. He yanked a comb through his hair. The comb snagged and pain burned his scalp. A pinprick compared to what he'd feel if they lost their chance at a baby. "We can still make it on time."

You'll notice I also changed the telling phrase *rushing to get dressed* into something we could see, and I added internal dialogue. As you move from showing to telling, your passages will get longer because you'll be adding in specific details and internal dialogue to help the reader understand what's happening. Length doesn't determine whether writing is good or bad. Content does.

As-You-Know-Bob Syndrome

This is an excerpt from my book *How to Write Dialogue: A Busy Writer's Guide.* I'm including it as an appendix here because of how closely related the issue of As-You-Know-Bob Syndrome is to the topic of showing and telling.

As the name suggests, As-You-Know-Bob Syndrome is when one character tells another character something they already know. It's done purely for the reader's benefit, and it's unnatural.

A character won't say something the character they're talking to already knows.

For example, a husband won't say to his wife, "When we bought this house two years ago, we emptied our savings for a down payment. We don't have anything left."

The wife already knows when the house was purchased. She knows they emptied their savings. She also knows they haven't been able to replace those savings yet.

Thus, her husband has no reason to say any of that.

Info dumps won't always be this obvious, but if you could add "as you know" to the front of whatever's being said, it's time to rewrite.

If it's common knowledge, it won't come up in conversation.

Let's say you have two sisters meeting to go out for lunch. One shows up at the other's door.

> "Come on in, Susie. I'm just cleaning up the muddy paw prints left by our pit bull Jasper."

It's common knowledge her sister owns a pit bull named Jasper. Her sister wouldn't feel the need to state it. She'd be more likely to say...

> "Come in for a sec. I just have to clean up the mud the stupid dog tracked in again."

Even essential information needs to be given in a natural way. So if knowing that their dog is a pit bull named Jasper is essential to the story, you could write...

> A flash of fur tore across Ellen's freshly washed floor and threw itself at Susie.
> Susie shoved the dog down. "Off, Jasper."
> He dropped onto his back for a belly rub, tongue lolling out of his mouth.
> Ellen sighed. "Sorry about that. Did he get you dirty?"
> Susie shook her head and scratched Jasper behind the ear. Even if he had, a little mud never hurt anyone. "Any

more trouble with the anti-pit bull crowd at the park? Brent said someone threatened to call the cops last week."

A character won't say something that isn't relevant to the conversation.

"A hundred years ago, when the dam was constructed, this town was built on the dried-out flood plain. If the dam breaks, it'll wipe out the whole place."

Did you catch the sneaky insertion of backstory in adding "a hundred years ago"? What normal person would actually say that? Who would care how long ago the dam was built when the real issue is whether or not the town is about to be destroyed?

If we have two town residents talking, they also know the town is built on a flood plain. While that's relevant to the conversation, it violates the common knowledge rule. Find a more creative way to bring in the information.

How can we avoid As-You-Know-Bob Syndrome?

Figure out what information is essential to the scene and only include that.

Let's look at an example where two brothers are being held captive. Their kidnapper leaves them locked in a room during the day while he goes to work.

"Remember the trick you used on Aunt Angie that summer we stayed with her? You rigged the doorknob so it wouldn't close securely when she tried to lock us in our room at night. We could do something like that."

This is an info dump because both characters already know the specifics. They'd be more likely to say...

"What if you did what you used to do to Aunt Angie?"

The problem is that's not enough info for the reader. So we pull out what's essential. When they were with Aunt Angie doesn't matter. Why she locked them up doesn't matter. What's really essential for the reader to know is that one brother knows how to rig a door so that even when it looks locked, it can actually be forced open.

"What if you did what you used to do to Aunt Angie?" Frank crinkled his forehead. "He never leaves us alone long enough. It took me a whole day to file the ridges off the doorknob latch."

But sometimes you really do need a character to talk about something they wouldn't normally talk about or to say something the listener already knows. What then?

Pick a fight.

Fighting characters will dredge up things the other character already knows and use them as weapons against each other.

Let's go back to our earlier example of the husband and wife (we'll call them Nathan and Linda) who bought the house two years ago, drained their savings, and haven't been able to replace their savings yet. Say we have a scene happening where the husband finally quit the high-paying job where he's treated like a doormat, but he did it without talking to his wife first. She's angry because they won't be able to make their mortgage payments on her salary alone.

Nathan balled up the resignation letter. "You're the one who wanted this house in the first place. I was happy in our apartment."

"We bumped into each other just trying to dress in the morning. We couldn't raise a family there."

"We could have waited at least. We shouldn't have rushed into a house and drained our savings. I wanted to stay in the job I loved."

"So it's all my fault?" Linda grabbed a club from his golf bag by the door. "We'd have plenty saved if you'd give up a golf game now and then."

Same information, much more exciting way of sharing it. (We also learn more about the characters and their relationship.)

Introduce a character to "play dumb."

A "dumb" character is one who's new to the situation and doesn't know what the others do. They don't actually have to be unintelligent. They can be highly intelligent in other areas. They just need to be out of their element or uneducated in this particular scenario. (Jeff Gerke, editor-in-chief of Marcher Lord Press, calls this a dump puppet.)

In the movie *Twister*, Dr. Melissa Reeves functions in this role because she doesn't know anything about tornadoes. She asks questions no other character would ask because they already know all about tornadoes. Through her, we learn the information we need to learn.

This was also part of the brilliance in how J.K. Rowling wrote her *Harry Potter* stories. Even though Harry was born from magical parents, he knew nothing of the magical world prior to coming to Hogwarts because he was raised by Muggles (non-magical folk). In other words, Harry learned about the world at the same time we did, and gave Rowling a natural, believable way to tell us what we needed to know.

Often you can also use a child in this role because children are naturally curious and haven't yet developed the social filter that holds many adults back. My best friend's seven-year-old daughter once said to another woman, "I love your skirt. It looks just like a towel." Children can get away with things that adults can't.

Other Books by Marcy Kennedy

For Writers

How to Write Dialogue

How do you properly format dialogue? How can you write dialogue unique to each of your characters? Is it okay to start a chapter with dialogue? Writers all agree that great dialogue helps make great fiction, but it's not as easy to write as it looks.

In *How to Write Dialogue: A Busy Writer's Guide* you'll learn

- how to format your dialogue,
- how to add variety to your dialogue so it's not always "on the nose,"
- when you should use dialogue and when you shouldn't,
- how to convey information through dialogue without falling prey to As-You-Know-Bob Syndrome,
- how to write dialogue unique to each of your characters,
- how to add tension to your dialogue,
- whether it's ever okay to start a chapter with dialogue,
- ways to handle contractions (or the lack thereof) in science fiction, fantasy, and historical fiction,

- tricks for handling dialect,
- and much more!

Each book in the *Busy Writer's Guides* series is intended to give you enough theory so that you can understand why things work and why they don't, but also enough examples to see how that theory looks in practice. In addition, they provide tips and exercises to help you take it to the pages of your own story with an editor's-eye view.

Strong Female Characters ⬚ ⬚ i⬚i⬚oo⬚⬚

The misconceptions around what writers mean when we talk about strong female characters make them one of the most difficult character types to write well. Do we have to strip away all femininity to make a female character strong? How do we keep a strong female character likeable? If we're writing historical fiction or science fiction or fantasy based on a historical culture, how far can we stray from the historical records when creating our female characters?

In *Strong Female Characters: A Busy Writer's Guide* you'll learn

- what "strong female characters" means,
- the keys to writing characters who don't match stereotypical male or female qualities,
- how to keep strong female characters likeable, and
- what roles women actually played in history.

How to Write Faster ⬚ ⬚ i⬚i⬚oo⬚⬚

In *How to Write Faster: A Busy Writer's Guide* you'll learn eight techniques that can help you double your word count in a way that's sustainable and doesn't sacrifice the quality of your writing in favor of quantity.

In our new digital era, writers are expected to produce multiple books and short stories a year, and to somehow still find time to build a platform through blogging and social media. We end up burning out or sacrificing time with our family and friends to keep up with what's being asked of us.

How to Write Faster provides you with tools and tips to help you find ways to write better, faster, and still have fun doing it, so that you'll have time left to spend on living life away from your computer. This book was written for writers who believe that there's more to life than just the words on the page and who want to find a better balance between the work they love and living a full life. The best way to do that is to be more productive in the writing time we have.

Fi☐tio☐

Frozen: Two Suspenseful Short Stories

Twisted sleepwalking.

A frozen goldfish in a plastic bag.

And a woman afraid she's losing her grip on reality.

"A Purple Elephant" is a suspense short story about grief and betrayal.

In "The Replacements," a prodigal returns home to find that her parents have started a new family, one with no room for her. This disturbing suspense short story is about the lengths to which we'll go to feel like we're wanted, and how we don't always see things the way they really are.

ABOUT THE AUTHOR

Marcy Kennedy is a speculative fiction and suspense writer who believes fantasy is more real than you think. It helps us see life in this world in a new way and gives us a safe place to explore problems that might otherwise be too difficult to face. Alongside her own writing, Marcy works as a freelance editor and teaches classes on craft and social media through WANA International.

She's also a proud Canadian, the proud wife of a former U.S. Marine, owns five cats and a dog who weighs as much as she does, and plays board games and the flute (not at the same time). Sadly, she's also addicted to coffee and jelly beans.

You can find her blogging about writing and about the place where real life meets science fiction, fantasy, and myth at www.marcykennedy.com. To sign up for her new-release mailing list, please visit her website. Not only will you hear about new releases before anyone else, but you'll also receive exclusive discounts and freebies. Your email address will never be shared and you can unsubscribe at any time.

Contact Marcy
Email: marcykennedy@gmail.com
Website: www.marcykennedy.com
Twitter: @MarcyKennedy
Facebook: www.facebook.com/MarcyKennedyAuthor

Printed in Great Britain
by Amazon